Warcraft®: The Sunwell Trilogy™
Written by Richard A. Knaak
Illustrated by Jae-Hwan Kim

Lettering and Layout - Rob Steen
Copy Editors - Peter Ahlstrom & Hope Donovan
Production Artists - James Dashiell and Jason Milligan
Artist Liaison - Eddie Yu
Cover Artist - Jae-Hwan Kim
Cover Design - James Lee

Editor - Rob Tokar
Digital Imaging Manager - Chris Buford
Production Manager - Jennifer Miller
Managing Editor - Lindsey Johnston
Editorial Director - Jeremy Ross
VP of Production - Ron Klamert
Publisher and E.I.C. - Mike Kiley
President and C.O.O. - John Parker
C.E.O. and Chief Creative Officer - Stuart Levy

A Manga

TOKYOPOP Inc.
5900 Wilshire Blvd. Suite 2000
Los Angeles, CA 90036

E-mail: info@TOKYOPOP.com
Come visit us online at www.TOKYOPOP.com

Special thanks to Chris Metzen, Lisa Pearce, Brian Hsieh, Gloria Soto, and Matt Kassan.

ISBN: 1-59532-713-4

First TOKYOPOP printing: March 2006
10 9 8 7 6 5 4 3 2 1
Printed in the USA

VOLUME 2
SHADOWS OF ICE

WRITTEN BY
RICHARD A. KNAAK

ILLUSTRATED BY
JAE-HWAN KIM

HAMBURG // LONDON // LOS ANGELES // TOKYO

HISTORY OF THE WORLD OF

The world of Azeroth has long been plagued by the misuse of magic. Originally, only dragons and night elves were able to practice the mystic arts, though eventually, even humans began to wield the unstable energy. Unfortunately, the unrestrained spell-casting eventually caught the attention of a malevolent, extra-dimensional force known as the Burning Legion.

The Burning Legion's first attempt to invade Azeroth, known as the War of the Ancients, was only thwarted after many lives were lost and the world's sole continent was shattered. With their second attempt, the Burning Legion used the Orcs from the world of Draenor as their pawns.

Twisted and corrupted by the Burning Legion's influence, the Orcs invaded Azeroth through the Dark Portal. After many ferocious battles, this Second War ended with the Orcs' defeat and imprisonment. Still determined to conquer Azeroth, the Burning Legion created one of its most twisted servants, the Lich King, to weaken Azeroth's defenders.

The Lich King spread a plague of death and terror across Azeroth that was meant to snuff out human civilization. All those who died from the dreaded plague would arise as the undead, and their spirits would be bound to the Lich King's iron will forever.

The army of the dead swept across the land, and Quel'Thalas, the glorious homeland of the high elves which had stood for thousands of years, was no more. The undead Scourge then moved south to Dalaran, and then to Kalimdor, home of the night elves.

Though the undead Scourge was stopped at Kalimdor, they had essentially transformed Lordaeron and Quel'Thalas into toxic Plaguelands. Grieving for the loss of their homeland, most of the high elves have adopted a new name and a new mission. Calling themselves blood elves, they now seek out and siphon magic from any available source, including demons.

Meanwhile, half of the undead forces staged a coup for control over the undead empire. Eventually, the banshee Sylvanas Windrunner and her rebel undead--known as the Forsaken--claimed the ruined capital city of Lordaeron as their own and vowed to drive the Scourge from the land.

Currently the Lich King resides in Northrend; he is rumored to be rebuilding the citadel of Icecrown. His trusted lieutenant, Kel'Thuzad, commands the Scourge in the Plaguelands. Sylvanas and her rebel Forsaken hold only the Tirisfal Glades, a small portion of the war-torn kingdom, while the humans, orcs, and night elves are trying to rebuild their societies

The story thus far...

Kalecgos, a young blue dragon, was sent by his master to investigate a strange surge of magical power. Before he could reach his destination, Kalec was shot down by the dragon hunter known as Harkyn Grymstone. Grymstone was a twisted, bitter dwarf who lost his loved ones in a dragon attack. He and his ragged band of hunters were only too happy to serve those who would enable them to slay all the dragons they could find.

Transforming into a humanoid form to escape the hunters' nets, a wounded Kalec was aided by Anveena, a kind, innocent maiden who lived nearby. Kalec tried to warn Anveena away, but she seemed unconcerned about the pursuing hunters. Even more remarkably, the young woman seemed unfazed by Kalec's true nature, though most people's reaction to meeting a dragon would be to flee or try to kill it.

Anveena's parents were equally welcoming to Kalec, and they maintained their friendly dispositions even when Grymstone kicked down their door. Kalec and Anveena used a hidden escape tunnel under the house to avoid the hunting party,

BUT THEY WERE DISCOVERED AND FORCED TO FLEE. KALEC TRANSFORMED BACK INTO A DRAGON AND FLEW AWAY WITH ANVEENA, BUT HIS WOUNDS AND GRYMSTONE'S ATTACKS DROVE HIM FROM THE SKY ONCE AGAIN.

UNABLE TO CONTROL HIS DESCENT, KALEC CRASHED INTO A NEARBY LAKE. ANVEENA SWAM TO SHORE AND FEARED THE WORST UNTIL SHE FOUND KALEC LYING AT THE WATER'S EDGE. LUCKILY, THE YOUNG DRAGON WAS ABLE TO TRANSFORM AGAIN AND WASH ASHORE BEFORE HIS BULKIER DRAGON FORM CAUSED HIM TO DROWN.

RETURNING TO ANVEENA'S HOME, KALEC AND ANVEENA FOUND ONLY BURNING WRECKAGE...AND THE UNDEAD SCOURGE. FIGHTING THE SHAMBLING CORPSES, KALEC AND ANVEENA WERE EASILY CAPTURED BY THE RENEGADE ELF KNOWN AS DAR'KHAN. DAR'KHAN PLACED PAIN-INDUCING MYSTICAL COLLARS AROUND KALEC AND ANVEENA'S NECKS, AND OFFERED THEM RELATIVELY PAINLESS DEATHS IN EXCHANGE FOR INFORMATION ABOUT THE SUNWELL.

THE SUNWELL WAS A POOL OF MYSTICAL ENERGY THAT WAS THE ESSENCE OF THE HIGH ELVES' LIVES. LOCATED IN THE ELVEN CITY OF QUEL'THALAS, THIS SOURCE OF MAGIC WAS AS

Kalecgos
A young blue dragon. Though trapped in humanoid form by a mystical collar Dar'Khan placed around his neck, Kalec retains many of his magical talents, including the ability to create a sword out of nothingness.

IMPORTANT TO THE ELVES AS EATING OR BREATHING. THEY USED ITS VAST POWER TO BUILD THEIR CITIES, MOLD THE LANDSCAPE AND MAKE WHATEVER THEY DESIRED. UNFORTUNATELY, DAR'KHAN DESIRED MUCH MORE THAN THE REST OF HIS BRETHREN, LEADING HIM TO AN UNHOLY PACT WITH ARTHAS, THE CORRUPTED HUMAN KNIGHT WHO BECAME THE LICH KING.

DAR'KHAN ENABLED THE UNDEAD SCOURGE TO BYPASS QUEL'THALAS' FABLED DEFENSES WHILE HE DRAINED THE SUNWELL'S ENERGIES. WHILE HIS PROUD HOME WAS OVERRUN BY VICIOUS, ZOMBIFIED CORPSES, AND DAR'KHAN FOUGHT HIS FELLOW ELVEN SORCERERS FOR CONTROL OF THE WELL, SOMETHING WENT HORRIBLY WRONG. THE SUNWELL'S POWER EXPLODED SPECTACULARLY, RAVAGING WHAT LITTLE REMAINED

Anveena
A caring, innocent young maiden. Anveena helped a wounded Kalecgos escape from dragon hunters, though her home and parents were destroyed.

UNTOUCHED BY THE SCOURGE.

DAR'KHAN WAS SAVED BY THE POWER
OF HIS DARK LORD, AND SENT ACROSS
THE CONTINENT IN SEARCH OF THE
SUNWELL'S ESCAPED MAGIC...WHICH
WOULD SEEM TO BE THE SAME POWER
THAT KALEC'S MASTER SENSED.
DAR'KHAN TRIED TORTURING KALEC
FOR INFORMATION, BUT HE WAS
INTERRUPTED BY THE ARRIVAL OF
TYRYGOSA, A FEMALE BLUE DRAGON
WHO IS ALSO KALEC'S INTENDED.
TOGETHER, TYRI AND KALEC MANAGED
TO WIPE OUT DAR'KHAN'S UNDEAD
SERVANTS AND DRIVE THE ELF AWAY...
BUT THEY COULD NOT REMOVE THE
COLLARS HE PLACED ON HIS TWO
CAPTIVES.

Tyrygosa
A female blue dragon and Kalec's
intended. When forced to assume a
humanoid shape, she refuses to look
merely human. In her words, "At least
elves are aesthetically pleasing."

SIFTING THROUGH THE SHATTERED TIMBERS OF ANVEENA'S
HOME IN SEARCH OF HER PARENTS, THE TRIO INSTEAD
DISCOVERED A STRANGE EGG, WHICH HOUSED AN EVEN
STRANGER WINGED SERPENT. ANVEENA NAMED HIM RAAC
(FOR THE NOISE HE MAKES) AND KALEC AND TYRI
SUSPECTED THAT THE BIZARRE CREATURE MIGHT HAVE
SOMETHING TO DO WITH THE SUNWELL ENERGY THAT
ATTRACTED THEM AND DAR'KHAN.

SINCE KALEC'S COLLAR PREVENTED HIM FROM
TRANSFORMING, TYRI CARRIED HER COMPANIONS TO THE
TOWN OF TARREN MILL IN SEARCH OF BOREL, A MAN WHO
ANVEENA'S PARENTS SPOKE OF OFTEN. THOUGH SHE NEVER
MET HIM, SHE BELIEVED HE MIGHT BE ABLE TO HELP
THEM REMOVE DAR'KHAN'S COLLARS. THE GROUP

Jorad Mace

A human paladin whose loyalty was sworn to Arthas...before Arthas betrayed his father, his homeland and his species. Mace is continually haunted by his terrible loss.

ATTRACTED A LOT OF ATTENTION IN THE SMALL TOWN, INCLUDING THAT OF JORAD MACE. MACE RECOGNIZED BOREL'S NAME, THOUGH HE WAS MORE INTERESTED IN HELPING ANVEENA ESCAPE THE TOWN THAN AIDING KALEC AND TYRI AGAINST A SURPRISE ATTACK BY HARKYN GRYMSTONE AND HIS FELLOW DRAGON HUNTERS.

GRYMSTONE HAD THE DRAGONS CORNERED WHEN HE SUDDENLY FOUND THAT HE, TOO, WAS SURROUNDED BY THE UNDEAD SCOURGE AND DAR'KHAN. DAR'KHAN REVEALED THAT HE HAD DISGUISED HIMSELF AS A HUMAN PRINCE TO PROVIDE THE VENGEFUL DWARF WITH THE RESOURCES NEEDED TO KILL ANY DRAGONS THAT MIGHT BE DRAWN TO THE AREA BY THE SUNWELL'S POWER. AS DAR'KHAN PREPARED TO TAKE RAAC FROM ANVEENA, A SURPRISE ATTACK FROM JORAD MACE HELPED THE DRAGONS AND DRAGON HUNTERS TURN THE TIDE.

WITH THEIR COMBINED EFFORTS, THE UNDEAD WERE WIPED OUT AND DAR'KHAN WAS CONSUMED IN A BLAST OF TYRI'S DRAGON

FIRE. WHEN MACE INFORMED THE OTHERS THAT THEY MIGHT FIND BOREL ON AERIE PEAK, AN APOLOGETIC HARKYN GRYMSTONE ADVISED THEM TO SEEK HIS COUSIN, LOGGI, WHO LIVES IN THE MOUNTAINS NEAR THERE.

HOPING THAT LOGGI MIGHT BE ABLE TO REMOVE THE MAGICAL COLLARS, KALEC, ANVEENA, TYRI AND JORAD MACE SEARCH NOT ONLY FOR THE DWARF, BUT ALSO FOR THE MYSTERIOUS BOREL, WHO MAY KNOW MORE ABOUT THE SUNWELL THAN ANYONE. HOWEVER, REACHING AERIE PEAK MAY BE HARDER THAN IMAGINED, EVEN WITH A DRAGON TO FLY THEM THERE...

OOMPH!

AAAARGH!

THWAM

RRRARGH!!

HNGH!

NNN...

OHH...

UNNNGH...
≷COUGH≷
≷COUGH≷

DAMN...

IT IS ICHOR WHO WIELDS AN ORB OF NER'ZHUL.

THE SCOURGE... THEY USE THE ORBS TO SUMMON THE GREAT DEAD...

...TO RAISE THE TERRIBLE BEASTS...

...LIKE THE FROST WYRM.

THE CREATURE YOU SAW WAS THE FIRST THE SCOURGE RAISED HERE, A THING STILL GROWING IN STRENGTH.

BUT THIS IS AN OLD LAND, A LAND OF MANY GREAT AND STRANGE BEASTS...AND ICHOR SEEKS MORE OF SUCH DEAD.

BUT THE FOUL CREATURE WILL *FAIL*, YOUNG TRAG-- YOU SHOULD TELL HER THAT!

CHAPTER TWO
BARON MORDIS

B-BOREL...

I SEE YOU ARE MUCH RECOVERED, GIRL...

...AND I SEE THAT THIS CHAMBER IS NOT AS SUITABLE FOR ONE SUCH AS YOU.

COME! IF YOU'RE WELL ENOUGH, THERE ARE BETTER PLACES IN THIS RUIN THAN THIS DANK ROOM.

I-I--

YOU STARE AT ME IN FEAR?

YOUNG TRAG, YOU'VE BEEN REMISS! YOU SHOULD'VE WARNED HER!

YOU FORCE ME INTO AN UNDESIRED SITUATION!

GOOD BARON, FORGIVE! WISHED HER TO EAT FIRST...

YOU SAW THE HINTS, GIRL, OF MY *CURSE*. YOU KNEW THE TRUTH IMMEDIATELY.

WHAT YOU FEAR IS NO MISTAKE! YOU KNOW ME FOR WHAT I AM...

...DEAD.

BEFORE YOU THINK IT, I AM *NOT* ONE OF THE SCOURGE, THOUGH THEIR MASTERS CURSED ME TO THIS UNDEATH.

YOUNG TRAG, WHO CAME TO MY REALM AS WANDERER AND STAYED AS A FRIEND, WILL VOUCH MY STORY.

A STORY BEGINNING WITH A LIFE FULL AND STRONG.

I, THE LAST OF MY HOUSE, TRIED TO RULE WITH THE KINDNESS AND CARE MY FOREBEARS HAD. FOR A TIME, I SUCCEEDED...

WE WERE SLAUGHTERED.

AS I LAY DYING, I WAS SICKENED BY WHAT THEY HAD DONE...

...BUT I KNEW THAT THEY COULD DO NO MORE TO ME, AT LEAST.

BUT I WAS WRONG...THE SCOURGE HAD USE OF ME.

EVEN DEATH COULD NOT STOP THEM...

...EVEN DEATH COULD NOT SAVE ME.

...HELPED US LAY WASTE TO THOSE GHOULS WE FOUND!

THERE WAS ONE WHO I HUNTED, BUT I NEVER CAUGHT...

...UNTIL A TRAIL LED US TO THE ALTERAC MOUNTAINS...

...AND UP INTO ITS COLDEST PEAKS...

...WHERE WE DISCOVERED THE FOUL GHOUL ICHOR CONDUCTING NEW HORROR!

HE HAD WITH HIM THE ORB OF NER'ZHUL...

...AND HAD COME IN SEARCH OF SOMETHING UPON WHICH TO USE ITS ACCURSED ABILITIES.

HE **FOUND** THAT
SOMETHING.

THAT WAS BUT A FEW DAYS AGO, GIRL.

IN THIS OLD PLACE, WHERE GHOSTS OF A DIFFERENT SORT WANDER, TRAG AND I'VE TRIED TO PLAN ON HOW TO SEIZE THE STONE AND *DESTROY* ICHOR BEFORE HIS EVIL GROWS ANY FURTHER.

BUT COME--

--I SAID THIS WAS NO PLACE FOR YOU!

TRAG-- SOME LIGHT!

WHAT-- WHAT WILL YOU DO ABOUT THE SCOURGE?

UNTIL TODAY, I WASN'T CERTAIN.

AGAINST WHAT THE *ARTIFACT* CAN DO, I AM *NOTHING*.

BUT NOW... NOW I HAVE THE HOPE OF SENDING HIM BACK TO THE HELL THAT SPAWNED HIM!

AND YOU SHALL HELP ME.

FLIK
FLIK

GAAHHH!

WOOOSH

I AM REALLY BEGINNING TO MISS WINGS!

THE FALL...IT MUST HAVE CAUSED AN AVALANCHE THAT SWEPT ME OUT OF THE CREVASSE...AND AWAY FROM THE SCOURGE!

OF COURSE, I'M LUCKY I WASN'T SUFFOCATED IN THE PROCESS...

AT LEAST THE SNOW SOFTENED THE LANDING...SOMEWHAT.

#RAAC!

YOU! I APPRECIATE THE HELP UP THERE!

RAAC!

BUT IF YOU'RE HERE WITH ME, THAT DOESN'T BODE WELL...

WE HAVE TO FIND THE OTHERS BEFORE THE SCOURGE DOES! IF ONLY...

WAIT...

...WHAT'S *THAT*?

RAAC!

A CAVE?

WE SHOULD TAKE A CLOSER LOOK--THEY MAY HAVE SOUGHT SHELTER INSIDE!

RAAC!

CHAPTER THREE
CAVERNS OF THE DEAD

CHIP CHIP

WHY ARE THEY TRYING TO FREE THE REMAINS OF THAT ANCIENT BEHEMOTH?

RAA--

THWUK

THWAM

SLAASSH

%+@#!!

HA!

HEH
HEH...

IT'S BEAUTIFUL... YET...

OMINOUS?

YES...

JORAD MACE...

JORAD MACE!

YOU MUST AWAKEN!

AWAKEN!

B-BOREL?

S-SO COLD... CAN'T MOVE...

HUFF
HUFF

DOES SHE LIVE?

I HEAR NOTHING... BUT SHE MUST!

CHAPTER FOUR

THE DWELLERS BENEATH

WHAT IS THIS?

RAAC!

BACK IN THERE WITH YOU, LITTLE ONE!

HMM? SAVE YOUR LIES...

LISTEN! I'M NO PAWN OF THE SCOURGE!

I WILL DEAL WITH THIS ONE! THE WORK MUST CONTINUE!

WE'VE NEARLY TWO OF THE BEASTS FREED AND ANOTHER HALFWAY...

THEY MUST BE READY FOR THE BARON!

ENOUGH TALK! BACK TO WORK!

UNGH!

BE SILENT, OUTSIDER!

IF YOU HOPE TO SAVE YOURSELF AND YOUR FRIENDS!

?!?

BIND THESSSE TWO!

THEY LIVE...FOR NOW...

I FIND THEIR PRESSSENCE CURIOUSSS...

SSSO CLOSSSE TO MORDISSS... HMM...

BRING THEM TO OUR OTHER PRISSSONER!

LET USSS SSSEE HOW HE REACTSSS!

ANVEENA...

ANVEENA...

ANVEENA...

GASP!

MY SINCEREST APOLOGIES, MY DEAR...

...ONCE AGAIN, I'VE FRIGHTENED YOU.

...WOULDN'T YOU?

I TRIED TO BRING HER HERE, BUT THE BARON IS WITH HER!

WHY SHOULD I BELIEVE ANYTHING YOU SAY? YOU SAID YOU'D HELP, THEN LEFT ME BOUND...

I SWEAR BY THE HONOR OF THE HIGHMOUNTAIN TRIBE! I WILL HELP YOU HELP FREE THE YOUNG FEMALE!

I STILL DON'T UNDERSTAND HOW SHE COULD BE ANY HELP WITH THIS ORB YOU SPOKE OF! SHE'S GOT NO MAGIC!

THE ORB OF NER'ZHUL TELLS THE BARON IT IS SO... NOTHING ELSE MATTERS...

WHETHER TRUE OR NOT, SHE WILL PERISH IF HE USES HER!

YOU SERVE HIM. WHY HELP US?

I DO NOT *SERVE!* I AM THE BARON'S *FRIEND!*

BUT THE BARON-- HE IS NO LONGER THE BARON... DESPITE THE LIES I TELL MYSELF.

BARON VALIMAR MORDIS IS MANY YEARS DEAD...AND WHAT WALKS NOW IS MORE MONSTROUS THAN THE SCOURGE.

WE CAME SEEKING METALS BADLY NEEDED FOR WEAPONS AGAINST THE SCOURGE, BUT WE FOUND INSTEAD THE BARON MORDIS.

THERE WERE SCOURGE IN THE MOUNTAINS, HE SAID, BUT HE HAD A WAY TO WIPE THEM OUT... AND MAYBE HELP BRING THE WAR TO THE PLAGUELANDS.

HE HAD AN ARTIFACT, STOLEN FROM THAT ONE, AND COULD RAISE GIANTS FROM THE DEAD.

THEY'D COME FOR MORDIS AND THE ORB, BUT I KEPT MUM. WOULDN'T BETRAY MY LADS OR THE BARON.

WE DUG 'EM UP, BUT I WENT OUT ONE DAY FOR AIR... AND WAS CAUGHT.

BUT THEN I SAW THE WYRM ATTACK YOU AND YOURS...AND I KNEW THAT THE BARON WAS FRIEND TO NO ONE.

THE SCOURGE HE MIGHT HATE, BUT SO DOES HE ALL LIFE.

A TERRIBLE TALE, MUCH LIKE OURS, WHICH YOU KNOW NOW. HERE WE CAME IN SEARCH OF YOU...

WELL... THAT WAS IMPRESSIVE, LASS.

FOUL SSSORCERESSS!

LEAVE HER BE!

OH, SHE I WILL... FOR NOW! YOU, THOUGH, I HAVE NO USSSE FOR--

WAIT! DON'T HARM THE LAD, AND I'LL SHOW YOU WHAT YOU'RE LOOKING FOR!

I'LL SHOW YOU WHERE MORDIS IS!

!!!

HMM?

I THINK...
IF I JUST HAVE
A LITTLE MORE
TIME--

HOW
FARE YOU
NOW,
TYRI?

I FEAR
WE MAY
NOT HAVE
THAT...

ISSS THAT
IT AHEAD? IF
YOU LIE--!

I'VE
NOT LIED,
BAG O' BONES.
THE END OF YOUR
HUNT LIES
THERE.

CHAPTER SIX
DEATH on the MOUNTAIN

ANVEENA-- LOOK!

IT'S THEM!

KRAK

THIS IS OUR CHANCE!

KLANK

COME ON!

KALEC! WATCH OUT!

HISSSSSSSAAA

FWOOSH!

THE *SCOURGE* AIN'T CONTROLLING THAT THING! IT MUST BE THE *BARON!!*

ANVEENA? ANVEENA!

YES... I CAN FEEL THE POWER...

THE GREAT BEASTS ARE WAKING, RISING TO MY COMMAND...

THE TUNNELS! THEY'RE CUT OFF!

THAT ⸮UNGH⸮ LEAVES ONLY ONE WAY--

WHAT'S HAPPENING IN THERE?

YES! ARISE, MY LEGION OF DEAD!

RUMBLE

TH-OOM

HHUUUU!

ARISE!

KRAK

GHAAA!

HISSSSSSAAa

YOU FOOL! DO YOU KNOW WHAT YOU'VE DONE?

!!!

KRAK

THE ORB IS RUINED! THE FROST WYRM CANNOT BE KEPT ANIMATED!

IT'S LOSING COHESION ABOVE US!

RELEASE ME! THERE'S STILL A CHANCE TO REANIMATE IT BEFORE IT FALLS ON THE CASTLE! I CAN--

NO, BARON...IT-- AND WE-- END HERE... NOW...

To be concluded in

Volume 3

GHOSTLANDS!

Dar'Khan ventures to the desolate plaguelands where once stood the elven city of Quel'Thalas...and the mighty Sunwell. The dark elf will stop at nothing to gain the power that was once almost his...but what role could Anveena play in his mad quest?

Kalec, Tyri, Jorad Mace and Raac are hot on their trail, but there are other forces in the ruins of Quel'Thalas--including a certain dark banshee queen--they must contend with before they can hope to thwart Dar'Khan.

The mysteries of Raac, the Sunwell and Kalec's quest will all be laid bare...and when all is revealed, nothing will be the same!

About the Creators

In addition to his work on *Warcraft: The Sunwell Trilogy* and *Ragnarok* (also by TOKYOPOP), Richard A. Knaak is the New York Times bestselling fantasy author of 27 novels and over a dozen short pieces, including *The Legend of Huma* and *Night of Blood* for Dragonlance and The Demon Soul for Warcraft. He has also written the popular Dragonrealm series and several independent pieces. His works have been published in several languages, most recently Russian, Turkish, Bulgarian, Chinese, Czech, German, and Spanish.

Those wishing to find out more about his projects or who would like to join his e-mail list for announcements should visit his website at http://www.sff.net/people/knaak

Jae-Hwan Kim was born in 1971 in Korea. His best-known manga works include *Rainbow*, *Combat Metal HeMoSoo*, and *Majeh*.

AVAILABLE NOW

WORLD OF WARCRAFT®
CYCLE OF HATRED

A new novel from Pocket Books
Available wherever books are sold

Also available as an eBook
www.SimonSays.com

TURN THE PAGE FOR A PREVIEW!

Byrok never imagined that the happiest time in his life would be when he went fishing.

On the face of it, it didn't seem to be the life for an orc. Fishing involved no battle, no glory, no challenging combat, no testing of one's mettle against an equal foe. No weaponry was involved, no blood was shed.

But it was less what he did than why he did it. Byrok went fishing because he was free.

As a youth, he had heard the false promises of Gul'dan and his Shadow Council who promised a new world where the sky was blue and the inhabitants easy prey for superior orc might to conquer. Byrok, along with the others of his clan, followed Gul'dan's instructions, never knowing that he and his council did the bidding of Sargeras and his foul demons, never realizing that the price for this new world would be their very souls.

It took a decade for the orcs to be defeated. Either they were enslaved by the demons they thought were their benefactors, or they were enslaved by the humans, who proved to have more fight in them than the demons imagined.

Demon magic had made Byrok's memories of his life in the orcs' native land dim. A lack of interest in remembering had had a similar effect on his recollections of his life in human bondage. He recalled mainly that the work was backbreaking and menial, and it destroyed what little of his spirit the demons had left intact.

Then Thrall came.

Everything changed then. The son of the great Durotan—whose death had, in many ways, been the end of the orcs' former way of life—Thrall had escaped his overseers and used the humans' own tactics against them. He reminded the orcs of their long-forgotten past.

On the day that Thrall and his growing army liberated Byrok, he swore that he would serve the young orc until one of them died.

So far, that death had not come, despite the finest efforts of human soldiers or demon hordes. One lesser member of the Burning Legion did, however, claim Byrok's right eye. In exchange, Byrok removed the demon's entire head.

When the fighting ended, and when the orcs settled in Durotar, Byrok requested that he be relieved of his service. Should the call to battle be sounded, Byrok promised he would be the first in line to take up the mantle of the warrior once again, even with one eye missing, but now he wished to make use of the freedom he had fought so hard for.

Thrall naturally granted it to him, and to all those who requested it.

Byrok did not need to fish, of course. Durotar included some excellent farmland. Since the human lands were located in the marshy territory to the south, humans could not grow crops, and so turned most of their energy to fishing. They would trade their surplus to the orcs in exchange for their surplus crops.

But Byrok wanted no fish caught by humans. He wanted nothing to do with humans if he could possibly avoid it. Yes, the humans had fought at the orcs' side against the Burning Legion, but that was an alliance of necessity. Humans were monsters, and Byrok wanted nothing to do with such uncivilized creatures.

So it was rather a shock to the one-eyed orc to find six humans in his usual fishing spot on Deadeye Shore.

For starters, the area surrounding Byrok's fishing hole was high grassland. Byrok's tracking skills had been reduced a bit by the lack of a good right eye, but he still saw no indication that any but he had traversed through the grasses—especially not any humans, who, for such small, lightweight creatures, were pathetically overt in their movements. Nor did Byrok see any airships nearby, nor any boats on the water within sight of the fishing spot.

How they arrived, though, was of considerably less concern to Byrok than the fact that they *had* arrived. Setting down his fishing gear, he unstrapped the morningstar from his back. The weapon had been a gift from Thrall after the Warchief had freed him from bondage, and Byrok went nowhere without it.

Were these fellow orcs in Byrok's spot, he would have questioned their presence, but humans—particularly human trespassers—deserved no such consideration. He would find out their intent by stealthier means. At best, they might simply be fools who strayed too far north and did not realize they were invading. Byrok had lived a long time, and had come to understand that stupidity was a far more common explanation than malice.

But at worst, these might be true invaders, and if they were, Byrok would not let them walk out of his fishing hole alive.

Byrok had learned the human language during his time in captivity, and so was able to understand the words of these six—at least those he could hear. From where he was crouched down amid the tall grass, he could hear only a few words.

The words he did hear, however, were not encouraging. "Overthrow" was one, "Thrall" another. So was "greenskin," a derogatory human term for orcs.

Then he caught the phrase, "We'll kill them all and take this continent for ourselves."

Another asked a question, the only word of which Byrok caught was "troll." The one who wished to take the continent then said, "We'll kill them, too."

Pushing aside the grass, Byrok looked more closely at the humans. He didn't notice anything particularly distinguishing about them—all humans looked alike to Byrok—but the old orc did notice that the two closest to him had the image of a burning sword on their person: one as a tattoo on his arm, the other as an earring.

His blood running cold, Byrok remembered where he'd seen that symbol before. It was long ago, when the orcs first came to this world at Gul'dan's urging: they called themselves the Burning Blade, and their armor and flags carried the same symbol that these two humans wore.

The Burning Blade were among the fiercest devotees of the Shadow Council. They were later wiped out, and none of that demon-loving clan remained.

Yet here were *humans* wearing their symbol, and speaking of killing Thrall.

His blood boiling, Byrok got to his feet and started running toward the sextet, twirling the morningstar over his head. Even with his bulk, the only noise he made as he approached was the whizzing sound of the morningstar's chain as it pivoted on the handle in Byrok's fingers and rotated along with the large spiked ball on the other end around the orc's head.

That was, unfortunately, enough. Two of the humans—the two with the Burning Blade symbol—whirled around. So Byrok targeted the nearest of those two first, throwing the morningstar right at his shaved head. He wasn't concerned about losing his weapon—no human could lift the thing, so it would be safe until he could grab it again.

"An orc!"

" 'Bout time one showed up!"

"Kill it!"

Since the element of surprise was gone, he let out a huge roar—that always intimidated humans—and leapt at another, this one with a full beard. Byrok's massive fist collided with the bearded one's head.

The one with the shaved head clutched his shoulder—he had managed to avoid being hit in the head, to Byrok's disappointment—and tried to lift the morningstar with his other hand. Had he time, Byrok would have laughed.

However, he was too busy grabbing another human's head in his right hand and preparing to throw the invader into one of his comrades. That did not happen, however, as another human attacked from the right.

Cursing himself for forgetting to account for the fact that he was now blind on that side, Byrok flailed out with his right arm, even as pain sliced into his side.

Two more humans piled on top of him, one punching him, the

other going at him with a blade. Byrok managed to step on one attacker's leg, breaking it instantly. The screams of his victim served to goad the orc, and he redoubled his attack. But there were simply too many of them. Even though two of them were badly injured, they continued to pile on him, and even Byrok could not defeat six humans while unarmed.

Realizing that he needed his weapon, he inhaled deeply and then let out a huge roar even as he punched both fists outward with all his strength. It only knocked his foes off him for an instant, but an instant was all he needed. He dove for his weapon, his fingers closing around the handle.

Before he could lift it, however, two of the humans pounded on his head, and another drove a dagger through his left thigh. Byrok flailed his arm outward, the morningstar's ball sailing through the air, just missing the humans.

Then, much as he loathed himself for being forced to do it, Byrok ran.

It was a hard thing for him, and not just because the dagger that was still protruding from his thigh slowed his gait. To run from battle was shameful. But Byrok knew he had a higher duty to perform—the Burning Blade had returned, only this time they were humans. And *all* the attackers, not just the two he'd noticed before, wore that flaming sword image somewhere on them: a necklace, a tattoo, *something*.

This was information that needed to get back to Thrall.

So Byrok ran.

Or, rather, he hobbled. His wounds were taking their toll. It became a struggle even to breathe.

But still he ran.

Dimly, he registered that the six humans were giving chase, but he couldn't afford to pay attention to that. He had to get back to Orgrimmar and tell Thrall what was happening. Even with his injury, his strides were greater than those of the humans, and he could outrun them. Once he pulled far enough ahead, he would lose them in the underbrush of this land that he knew better than any outsider possibly could. Besides, they only seemed to want to beat up an orc. They probably did not realize that Byrok understood their gutter tongue, and therefore they did not know that Byrok knew who they were. They would not chase him past the point where it would be useful to them.

Or so he hoped.

No longer were there any thoughts in Byrok's mind. He cleared his head of all save the critical imperative of putting one foot down in front of the other, the ground slamming into his soles. He ignored the pain in his leg, and in all the other places they'd beat or cut him, ignored the fact that his one good eye was getting foggy, ignored the fatigue that drained the strength from his limbs.

Still he ran.

Then he stumbled. His left leg refused to lift as it was supposed to— but his right leg continued to run, and so he crashed to the ground, high grass and dirt getting in his nose and mouth and eye.

"Must . . . get . . . up . . ."

"You ain't goin' nowhere, monster." Byrok could hear the voice, hear the humans' footfalls, and then feel the pressure when two of them sat on his back, immobilizing him. " 'Cause, here's the thing— your time is over. Orcs don't belong in this world, and so we're gonna take you out of it. Got me?"

Byrok managed the effort of lifting his head so he could see two of the humans. He spat at them.

The humans just laughed. "Let's do it, boys. *Galtak Ered'nash!*"

The other five all replied in kind: "*Galtak Ered'nash!*" Then they started beating the orc.

NO. I'D RATHER KILL RATS.

Enter the World of Warcraft® and join thousands of mighty heroes in an online world of myth, magic and legendary adventure. Jagged snowy peaks, mountain fortresses, harsh winding canyons. Zeppelins flying over smoldering battlefields, epic sieges: an infinity of experiences await. Will you fight rats? No. Will you have fun? Yes, m'Lord. We didn't hold anything back in creating the World of Warcraft®. And now there's nothing holding you back. Visit www.worldofwarcraft.com today for more

MASSIVELY EPIC ONLINE

LIFE
BY KEIKO SUENOBU

Ordinary high school teenagers...
Except that they're not.

LIFE™

READ THE ENTIRE FIRST CHAPTER ONLINE FOR FREE:

Ayumu struggles with her studies, and the all-important high school entrance exams are approaching. Fortunately, she has help from her best bud Shii-chan, who is at the top of the class. But when the test results come back, the friends are surprised: Ayumu surpasses Shii-chan's scores and gets into the school of her choice—without Shii-chan! Losing her friend is so painful for Ayumu that she starts cutting herself to ease her sorrow. Finally, Ayumu seeks comfort in a new friend, Manami. But will Manami prove to be the friend that Ayumu truly needs? Or will Ayumu continue down a dark path?

LIFE Volume 1
Keiko Suenobu

It's about real teenagers...

It's about real high school...

It's about real life.

BIZENGHAST

Dear Diary,
I'm starting to feel

that I'm not like other people...

THIS FALL, TOKYOPOP CREATES A FRESH, NEW CHAPTER IN TEEN NOVELS...

For Adventurers...

Witches' Forest:
The Adventures of Duan Surk

By Mishio Fukazawa
Duan Surk is a 16-year-old Level 2 fighter who embarks on the quest of a lifetime—battling mythical creatures and outwitting evil sorceresses, all in an impossible rescue mission in the spooky Witches' Forest!

BASED ON THE FAMOUS
FORTUNE QUEST WORLD

For Dreamers...

Magic Moon

By Wolfgang and Heike Hohlbein
Kim enters the enigmatic realm of Magic Moon, where he battles unthinkable monsters and fantastical creatures—in order to unravel the secret that keeps his sister locked in a coma.

THE WORLDWIDE BESTSELLING FANTASY
THRILLOGY ARRIVES IN THE U.S.!

RAGNAROK